Sophia Gets a Bible

Kristyn Perez

www.thedailygraceco.com

Unless otherwise noted, Scripture quotations have been taken from the Christian Standard Bible®, Copyright © 2020 by Holman Bible Publishers. Used by permission. Christian Standard Bible® and CSB® are federally registered trademarks of Holman Bible Publishers.

Designed in the United States of America and printed in China.

STUDY CONTRIBUTORS

Illustrator:
KATIE GRACE WILL

Editors:
JENNIE HEIDEMAN
HELEN HUMMEL
ALLI MCDOUGAL

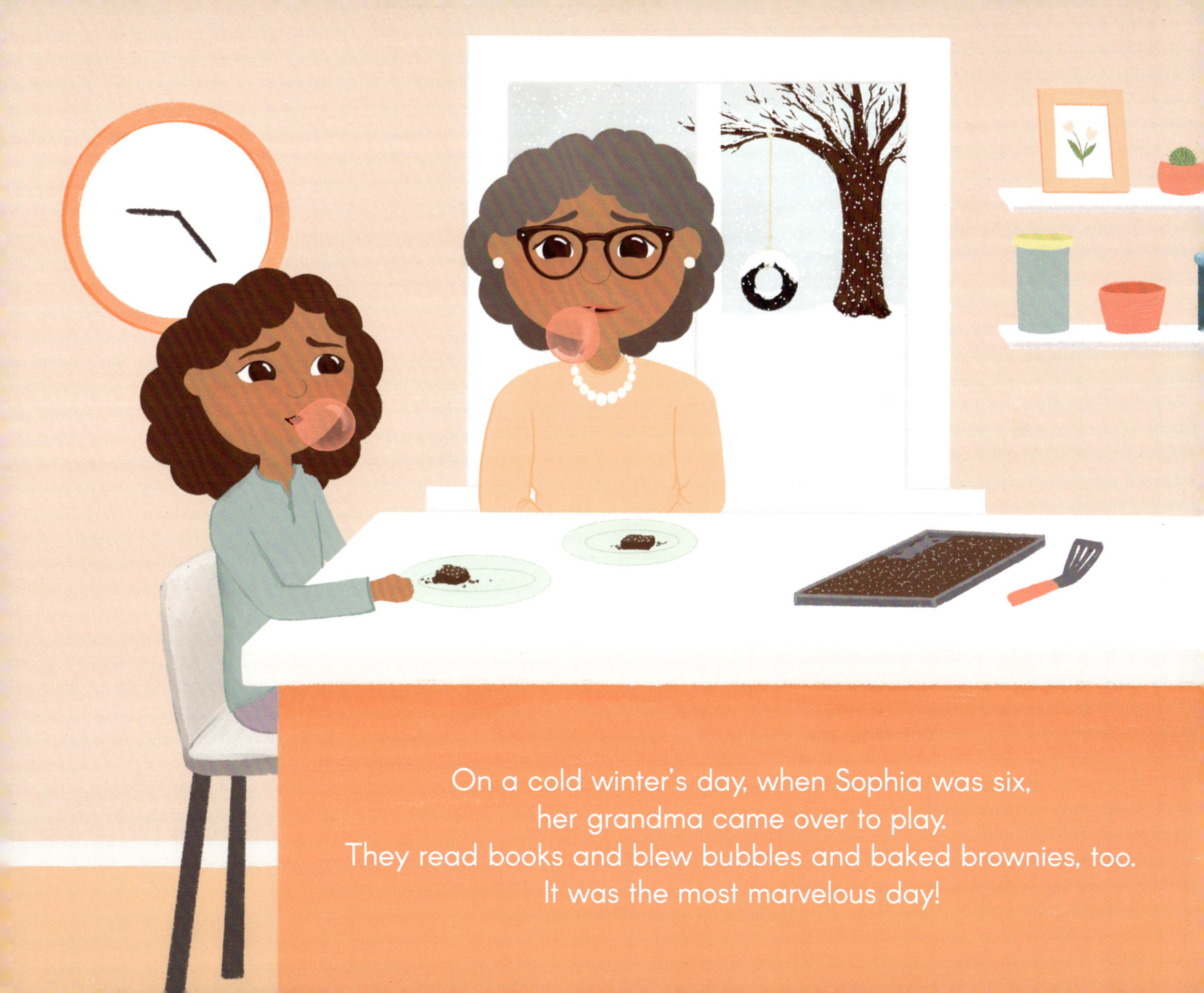

On a cold winter's day, when Sophia was six,
her grandma came over to play.
They read books and blew bubbles and baked brownies, too.
It was the most marvelous day!

But, throughout it all, Sophia kept eyeing
the present that sat by the fire.
It was glittering pink and topped with a bow,
with a sparkling tag she admired.

She thought she could spot Grandma's wonderful note
on the shimmering tag sitting there.
It looked like a big sweeping "S" just for her!
Should she peek? No, she didn't dare.

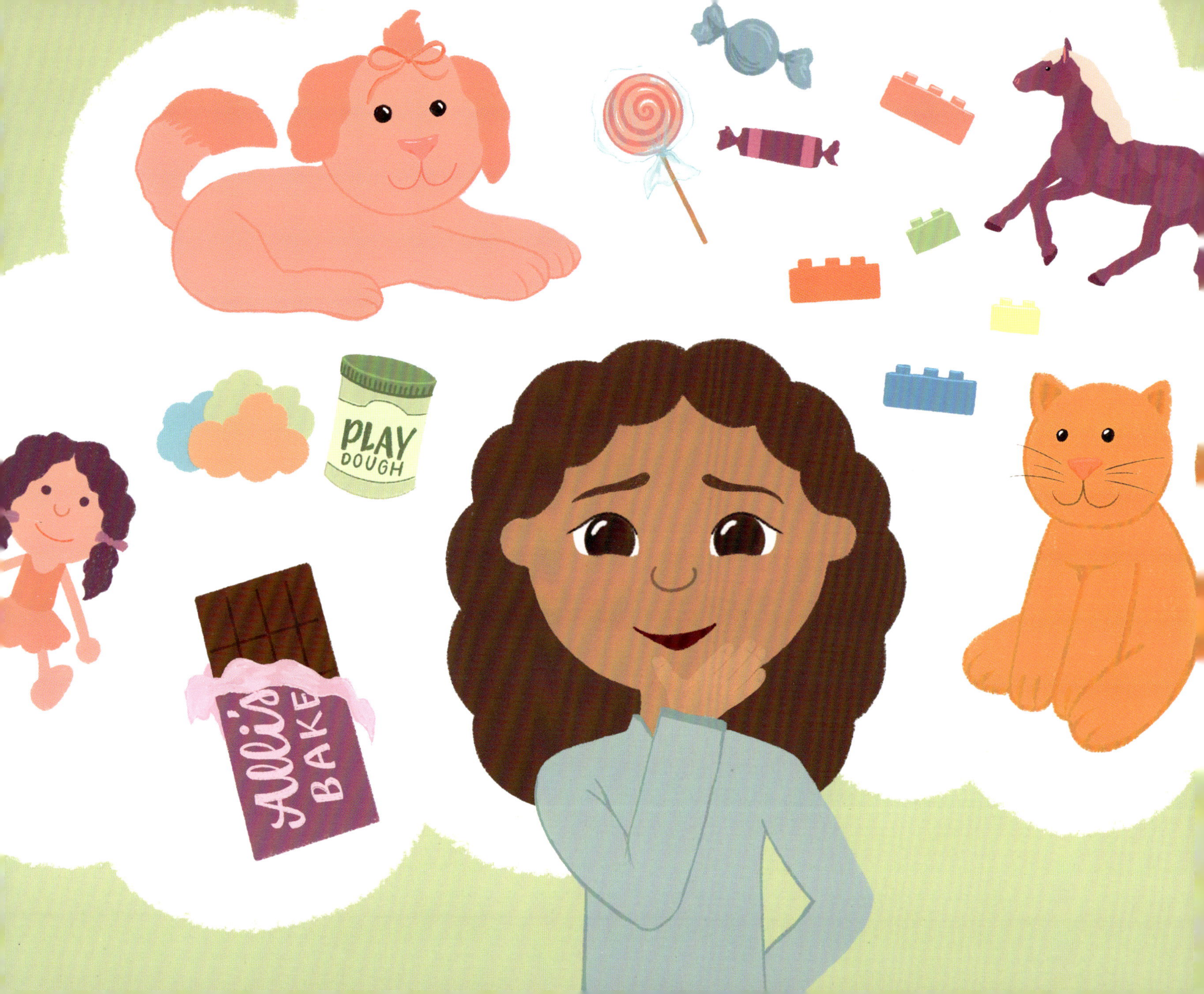
PLAY
DOUGH
Alli's
BAKE

Was the present for her? She'd try to ignore it.
She tried... but she just couldn't stop.
What was hidden inside? Was it something she'd like?
Was it chocolate from Alli's Bakeshop?

Was it playdough or a plush pink puppy?
Was it candy or maybe a cat?
Was it building blocks, baby dolls, or bouncing balls?
A horse or maybe a hat?

Then after lunch,
her grandma came closer
and said that she
had a surprise.

She asked sweet Sophia to sit on the couch,
to scooch over and cover her eyes.

Sophia heard rustling and then felt the box,
as it playfully plonked on her lap.
"Now, open your eyes!" her grandma cheered loudly.
"The time has come! Ready... set... unwrap!"

Full of excitement, she tore off the paper.
Her smile stretched from ear to ear.
She yanked at the paper with big tugs of joy
'til a book began to appear!

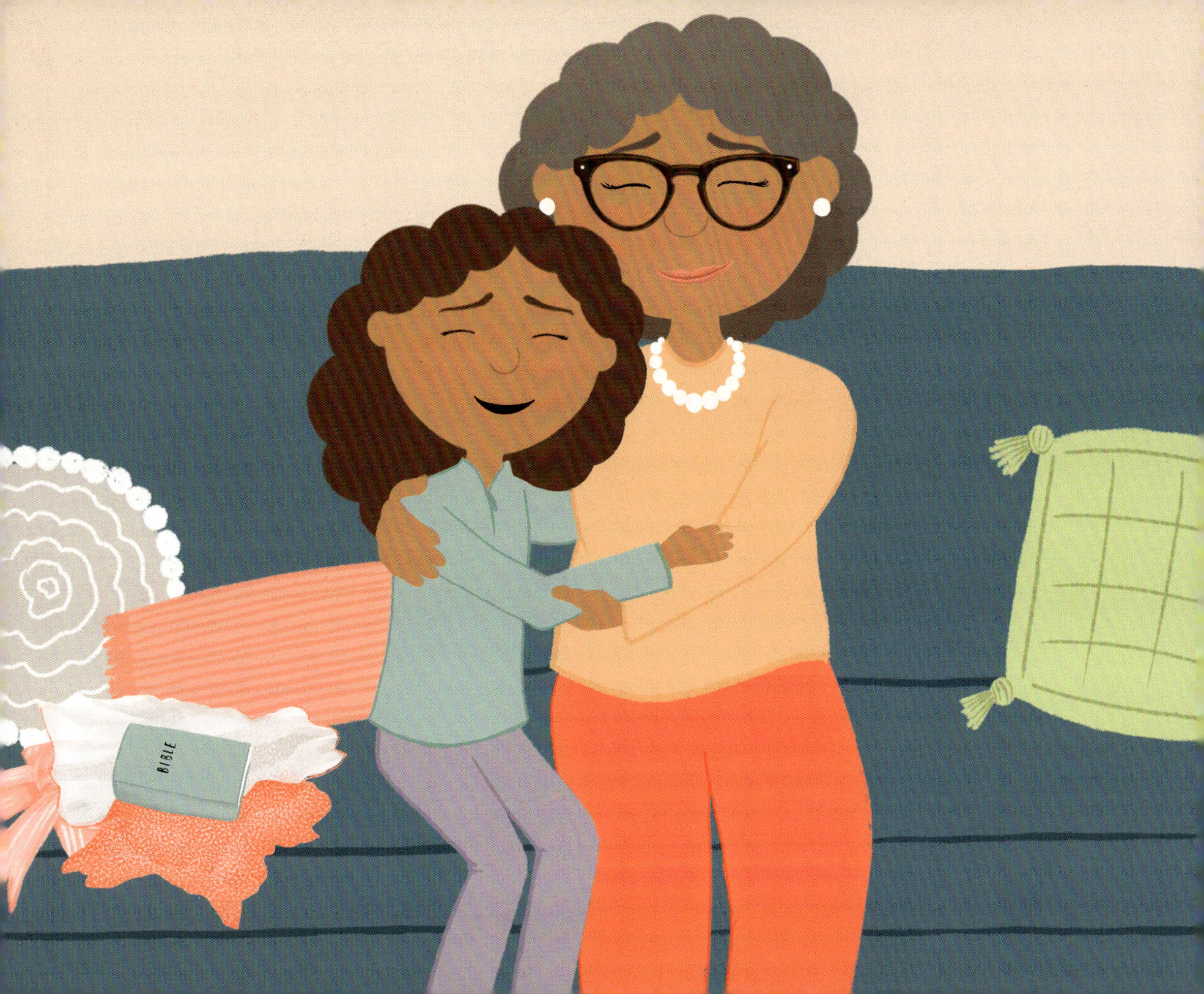
BIBLE

"This is *your* Bible—your very first one,"
her grandma then said cheerfully.
"Now tell me, Sophia, what do you think?"
"I *love* it!" she giggled with glee.

Her grandma said beaming,
"Your mom said you're reading,
and this book's the best that there is."
Full of excitement, Sophia said brightly,
"I can't wait to read what it says!"

Sophia then asked, "So how do I read it?
Do I read from beginning to end?
Do I read it like one of my chapter books?
Are the words real, or are they pretend?"

Before Grandma could answer,
Sophia continued,
"And why are there so many pages?
There's so much to read here
and some really big names.
Reading this will take me ages!"

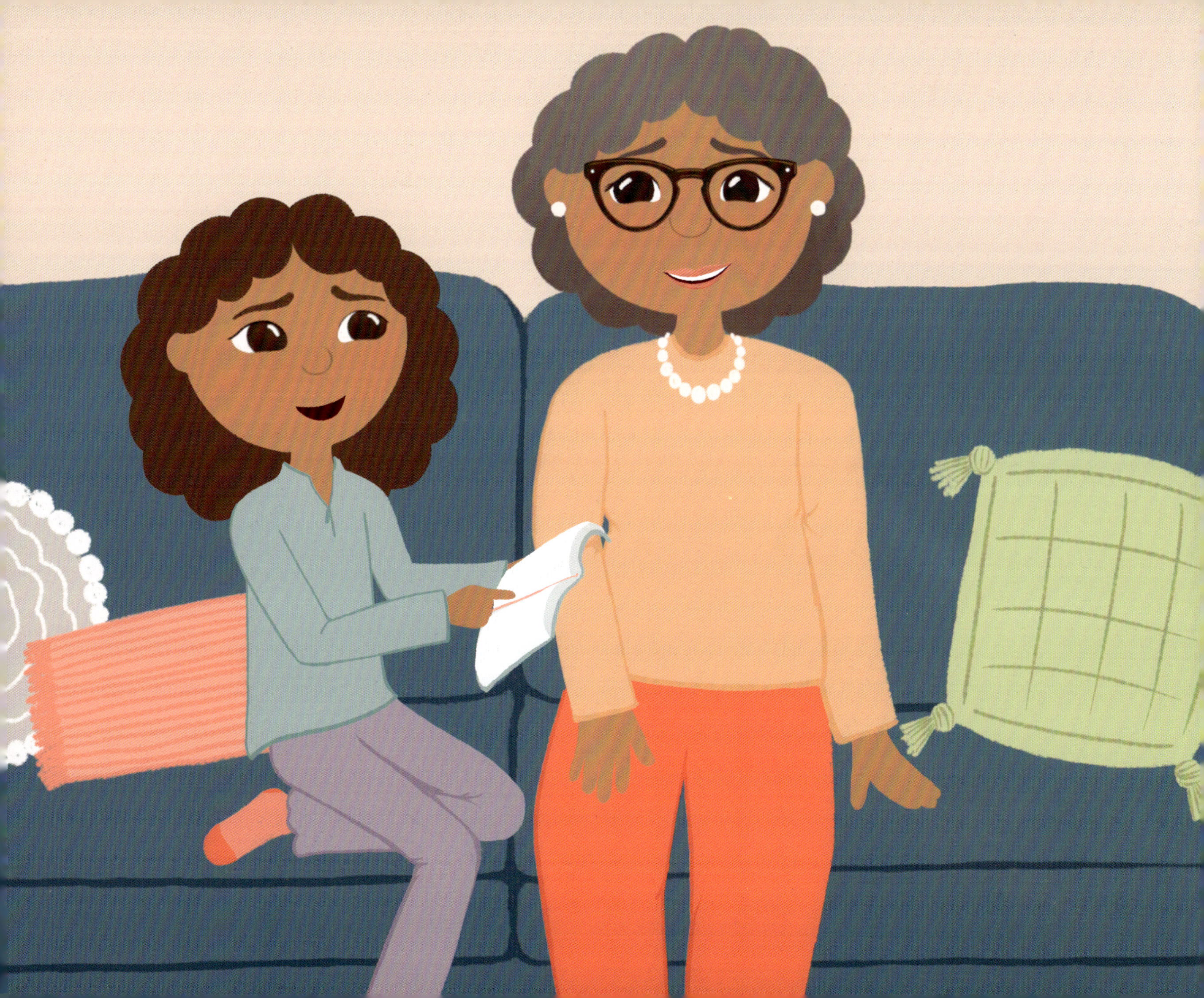

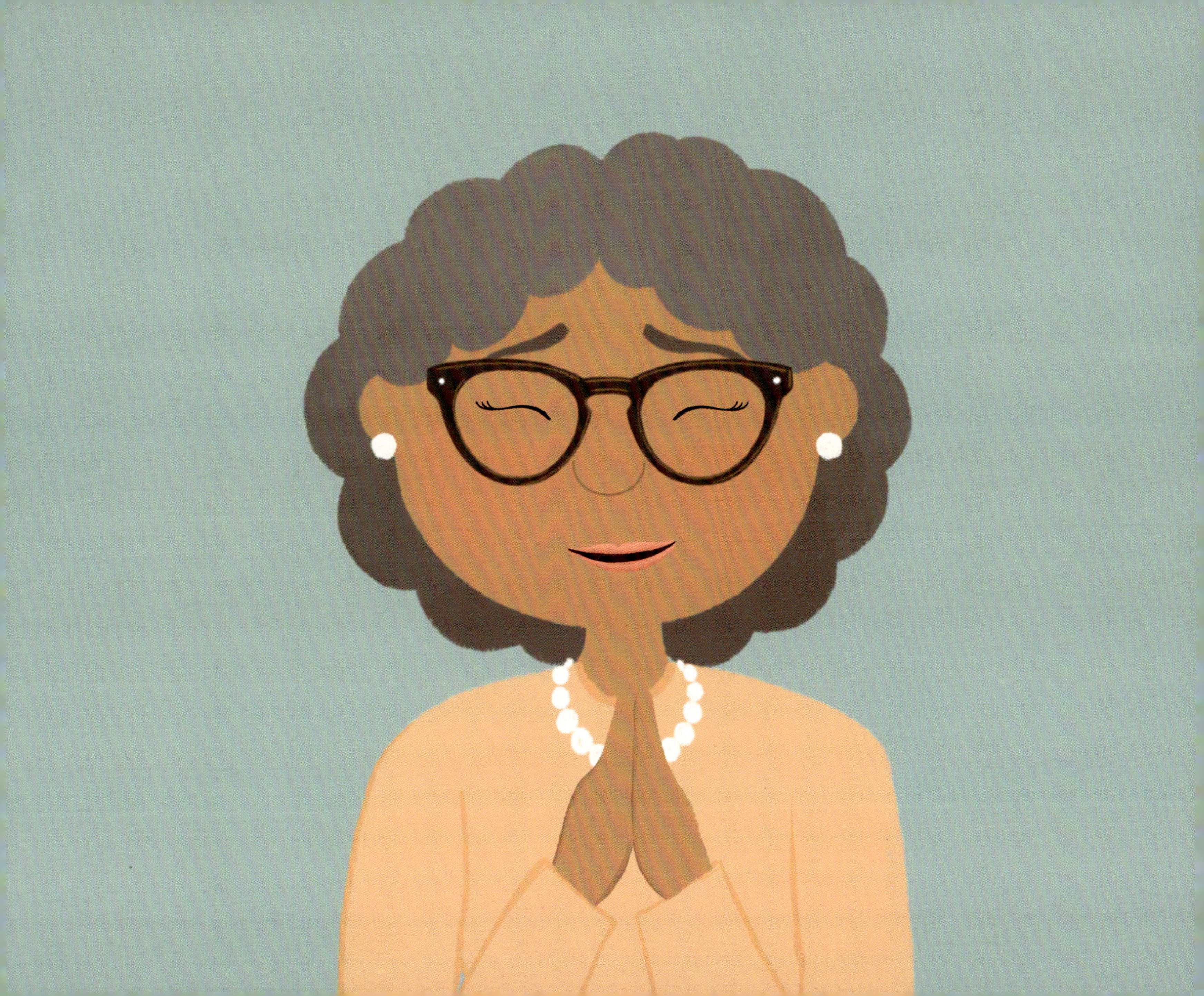

Sophia's sweet grandma then snuggled in closer,
excited to share from her heart
about her awesome God and His trustworthy Word
and the joy that she hoped to impart.

She paused for a second and whispered a prayer.
"Dear Lord, please guide my words as I speak,
and help me to say what is true, right, and good.
God, may it be You Sophia seeks."

She looked at Sophia with brown eyes aglitter,
the Bible laid over her lap.
And she started to share the good news of God's Word,
the gospel of Jesus, recapped.

"First, let me say how excited I am
to be reading this book with you!
The Bible's my favorite; it's changed my life!
It helps me and comforts me too."

"I've read the Bible for fifty-five years.
And each day I learn something new.
The whole Bible points to Jesus, God's Son.
Every word is faithful and true."

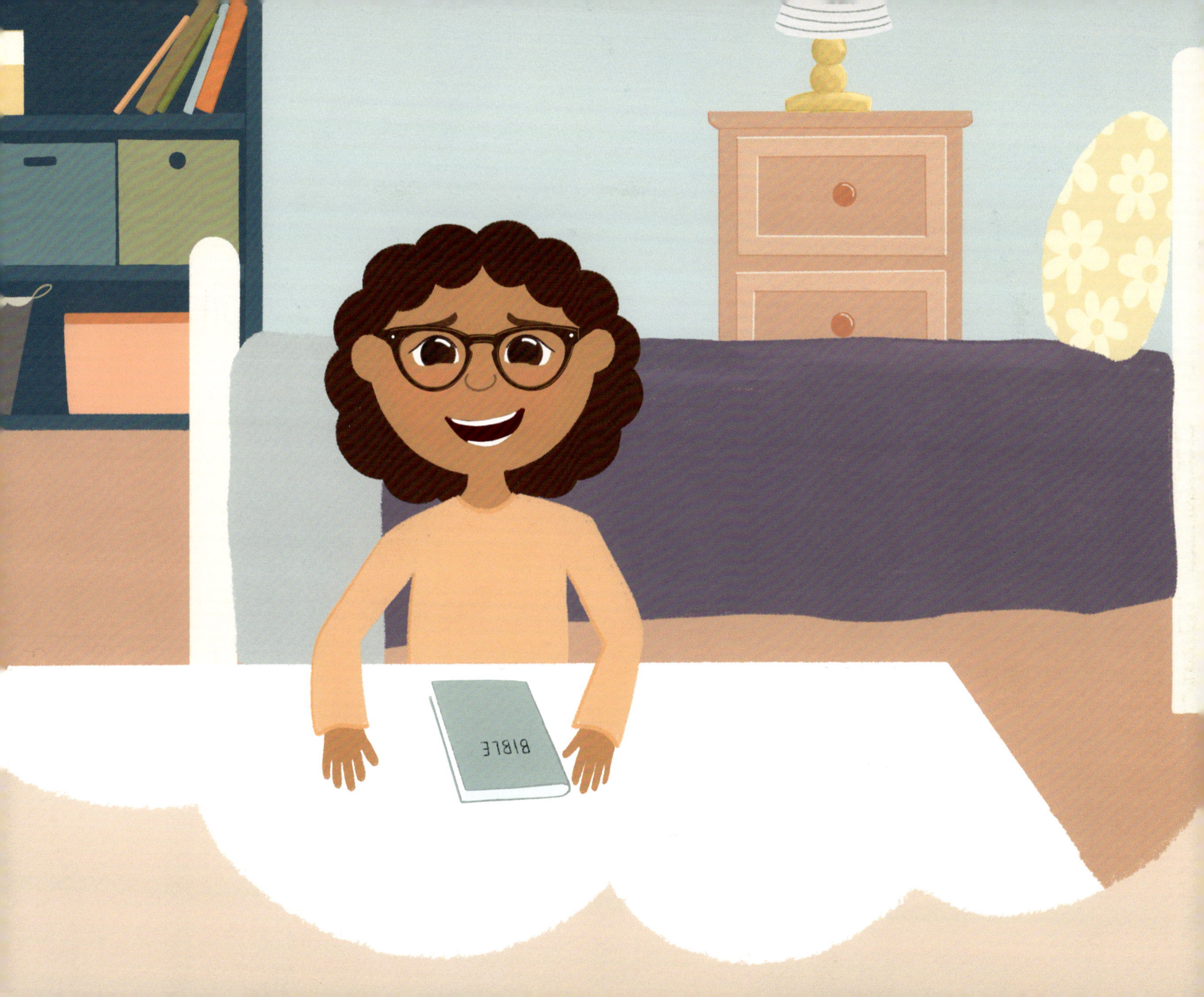
BIBLE

GENESIS
EXODUS
LEVITICUS
NUMBERS
DEUTERONOMY
JOSHUA
JUDGES
RUTH
1 SAMUEL
2 SAMUEL
1 KINGS
2 KINGS
1 CHRONICLES
2 CHRONICLES
EZRA
JOB
PSALMS
Proverbs
ECCLESIASTES
Song of Solomon
ISAIAH
JEREMIAH
Lamentations
EZEKIEL
DANIEL
HOSEA
JOEL
amos
OBADIAH
Jonah
MICAH
Nahum
HABAKKUK
Zephaniah
Haggai
Zechariah
MALACHI
Matthew
MARK
Luke
JOHN
Acts
ROMANS
1 CORINTHIANS
2 CORINTHIANS
Galatians
EPHESIANS
Philippians
Colossians
1 THESSALONIANS
2 THESSALONIANS
1 TIMOTHY
2 TIMOTHY
Titus
Philemon
HEBREWS
JAMES
1 PETER
2 PETER
1 John
2 John
3 John
JUDE
Revelation

"The Bible is one book divided in parts;
it has sixty-six books in all.
It starts with creation when God made the world,
and then, it describes the Fall."

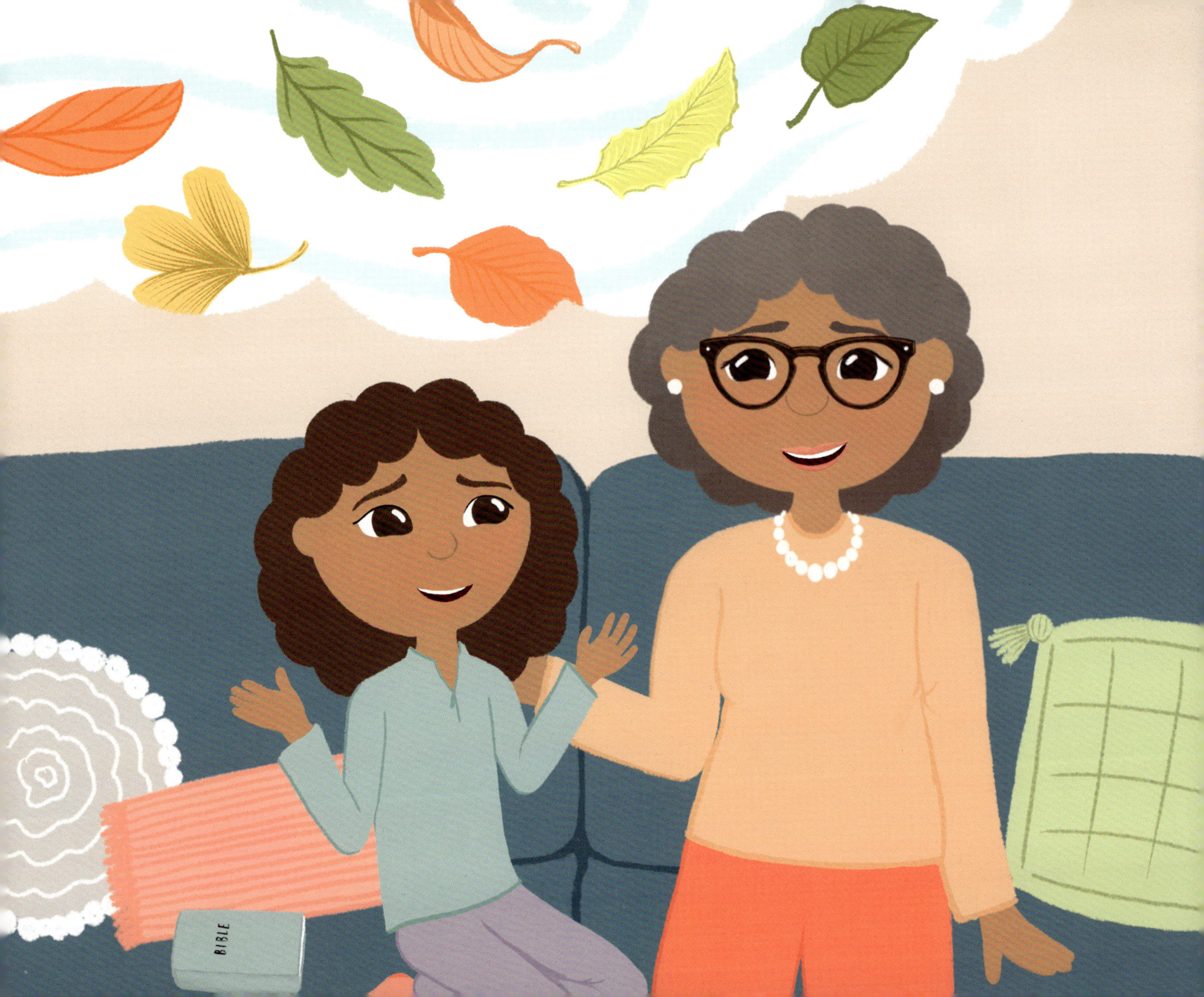
BIBLE

"What is the Fall?" Sophia asked slowly.
"I think I've heard of it before.
Is it 'fall' like the season? Like winter or spring?
Or 'fall' like a drop to the floor?"

Her grandma then smiled and pulled her in closer.
"Sophia, you have a great mind!
I love that you ask such thoughtful questions.
You're smart, creative, and kind."

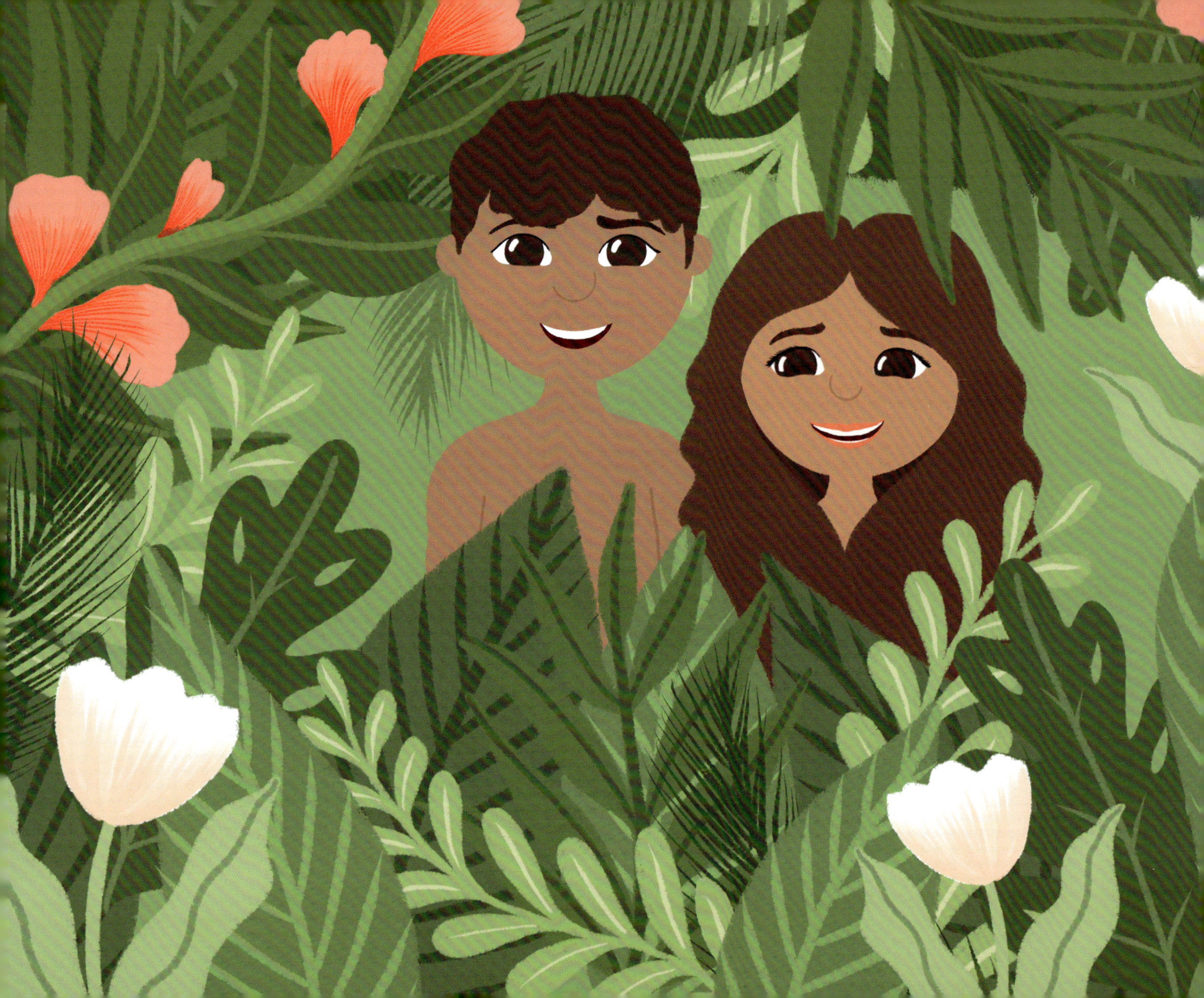

"When God made the world, He made it perfect;
there was no sin, and there was no shame.
But Satan entered God's beautiful world
and to the first people, made a false claim."

"Satan told them they could eat from a tree,
though God had said to stay away.
God had good intentions for His people,
but they were led astray."

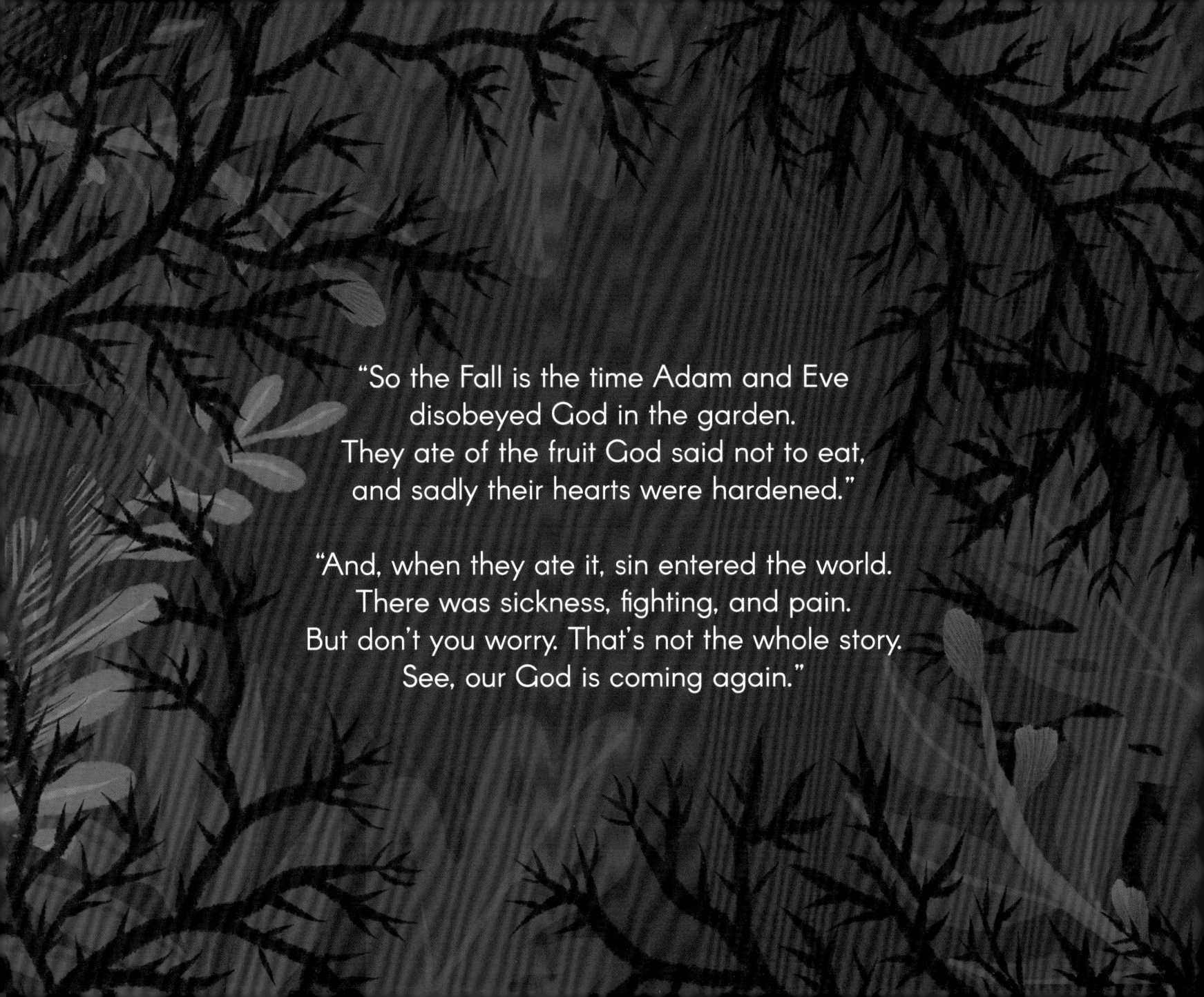

"So the Fall is the time Adam and Eve
disobeyed God in the garden.
They ate of the fruit God said not to eat,
and sadly their hearts were hardened."

"And, when they ate it, sin entered the world.
There was sickness, fighting, and pain.
But don't you worry. That's not the whole story.
See, our God is coming again."

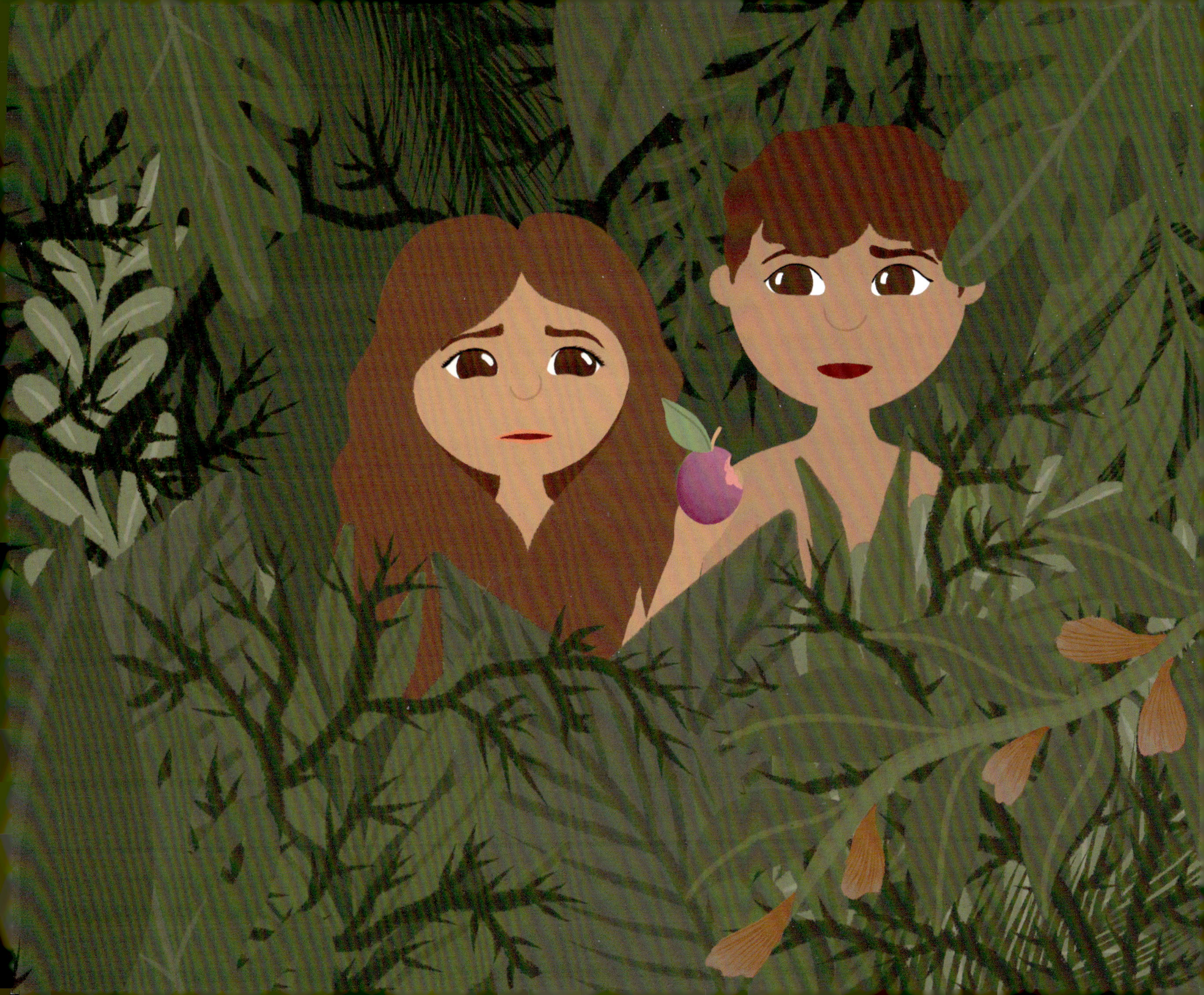

"God didn't want us to hurt or be sad,
to sin or be stuck in our fears.
He made the world good, and He gives us peace.
He cares for our boo-boos and tears."

"And God had a plan to make everything right,
to bring light to a world that was dim.
God sent His Son Jesus to rescue the world,
to save all who would put trust in Him."

"Jesus came as a baby, a boy and yet God.
He was perfect—from head to toe.
He was loving and kind, gentle and good,
the best friend we ever could know."

"Did you know that Jesus lived without sin?
He never once cheated or lied.
He never stole from His brother or yelled at His mother,
He never had envy or pride."

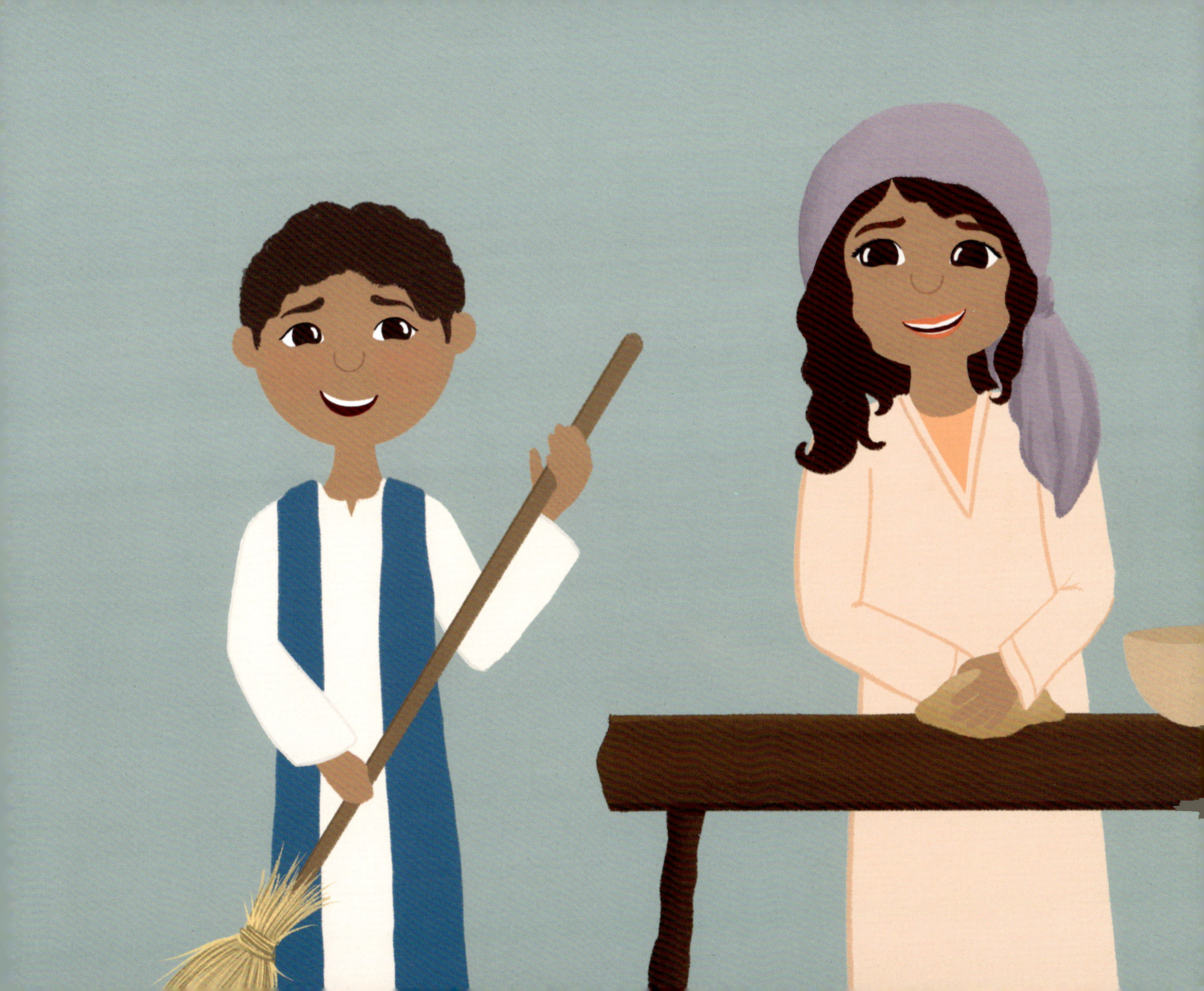

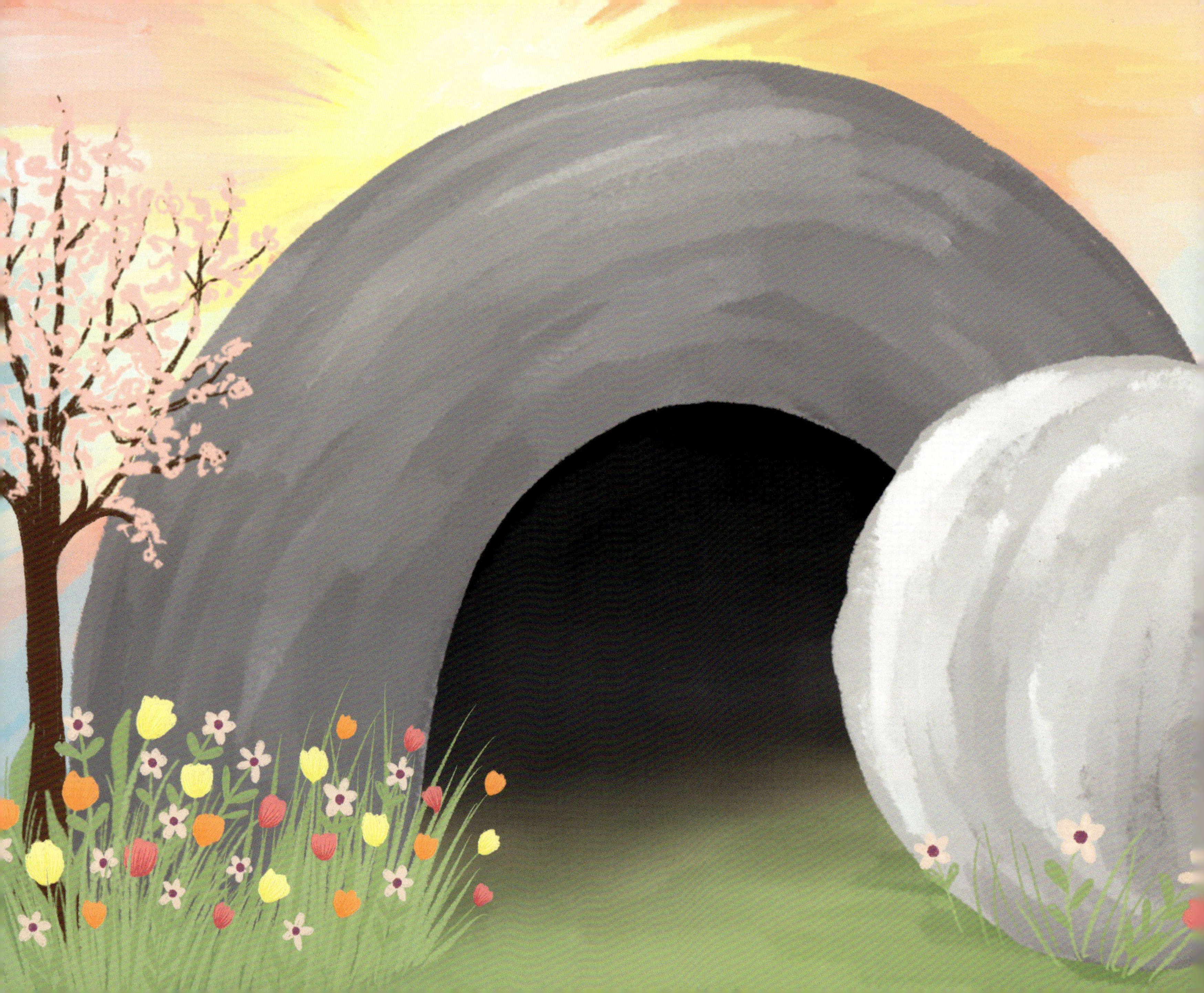

"And, not only this, but He loves us, too!
He died on the cross for our sins.
He took our punishment and took our place.
But then, came alive once again!"

"And one day He's coming to make all things right.
There will be no more band-aids or tears.
There'll be no more mean words or 'sorrys' or scares.
There'll be no more anger or fears."

"We read the Bible to learn about God. It is **trustworthy, timeless, and TRUE.**

God left us His book to share what He loves, how to KNOW HIM and Worship Him too."

Sophia then smiled and looked up in awe.
"Oh, there's so much here for me to learn!"
Her grandma said, "I've had a lifetime of joy
in this Bible, and now it's your turn."

Sophia leaned in and gave Grandma a hug,
and together they started to read.
Throughout the years, her faith blossomed and grew,
thanks to Grandma, who planted the seed.

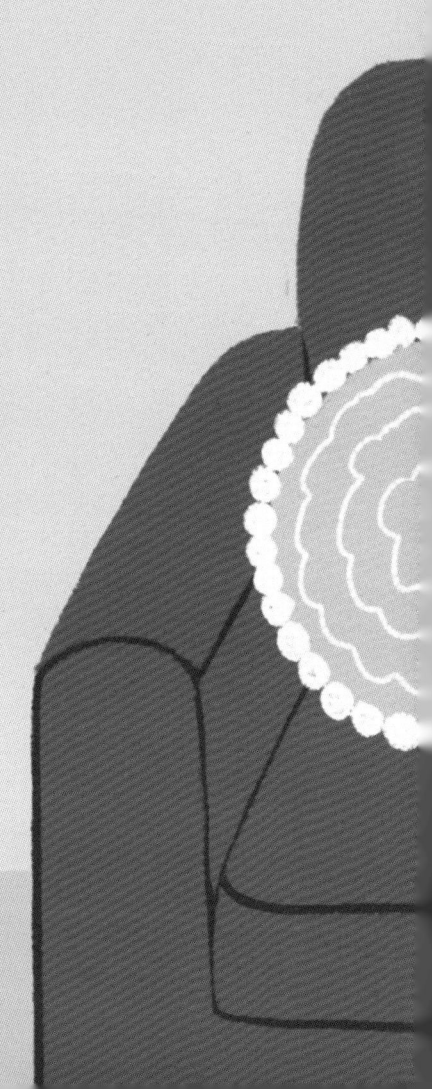

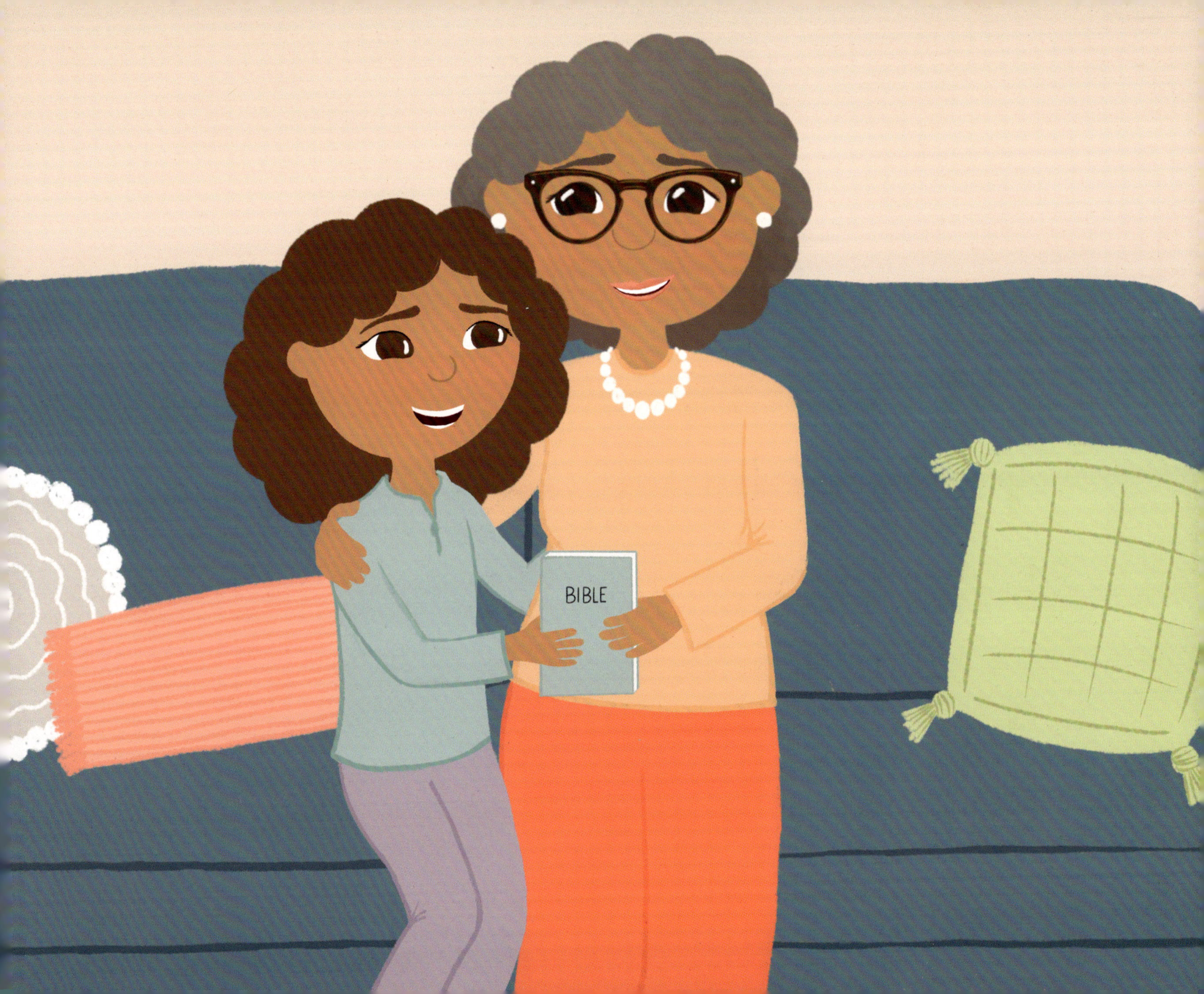
BIBLE

What is the Gospel?

THE WORD "GOSPEL" MEANS "GOOD NEWS."

The gospel is the most beautiful story in the whole world! God created the world and everything in it and made it good. He also made people, and He loved them very much.

BUT THE PEOPLE DISOBEYED GOD. THIS IS CALLED SIN.

We all disobey God, and the punishment for our sin is death. Thankfully, God had a plan from the beginning to save His people. We deserve to die for our sins, but the gospel says that God sent His Son, Jesus, to take our place. Jesus, who never sinned, died on the cross for us. Three days later, He came alive again! If we believe this good news and trust Jesus to save us, God forgives us, and we can live forever with Him.

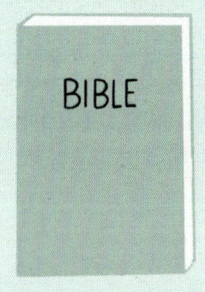

WHEN WE TRUST IN JESUS, GOD CHANGES OUR HEARTS.

He forgives us, makes us clean, and sends His Spirit to live inside us. He makes us His sons and daughters. He protects, loves, and cares for us. In response, we want to live in a way that makes Him happy. Doing good things doesn't save us. We don't obey God to make Him love us. He loves us always and forever! Instead, we obey God because we love Him.

WE CAN LEARN MORE ABOUT GOD AND WHAT HE LOVES THROUGH THE MOST IMPORTANT BOOK OF ALL, THE BIBLE.

The Bible tells us that one day, Jesus is coming again to make everything right. He will wipe away all our tears, and there will be no more pain or sadness. He will make everything good again.

If you trust in Jesus, don't keep this good news to yourself. Tell someone about Jesus today!

Thank You

for studying God's
Word with us!

connect with us
@THEDAILYGRACECO @DAILYGRACEPODCAST

contact us
INFO@THEDAILYGRACECO.COM

share
#THEDAILYGRACECO

visit us online
WWW.THEDAILYGRACECO.COM